Dd Ee Ff

Jj Kk Ll

Pp Qq Rr

Vv Ww

Zz

jet plane

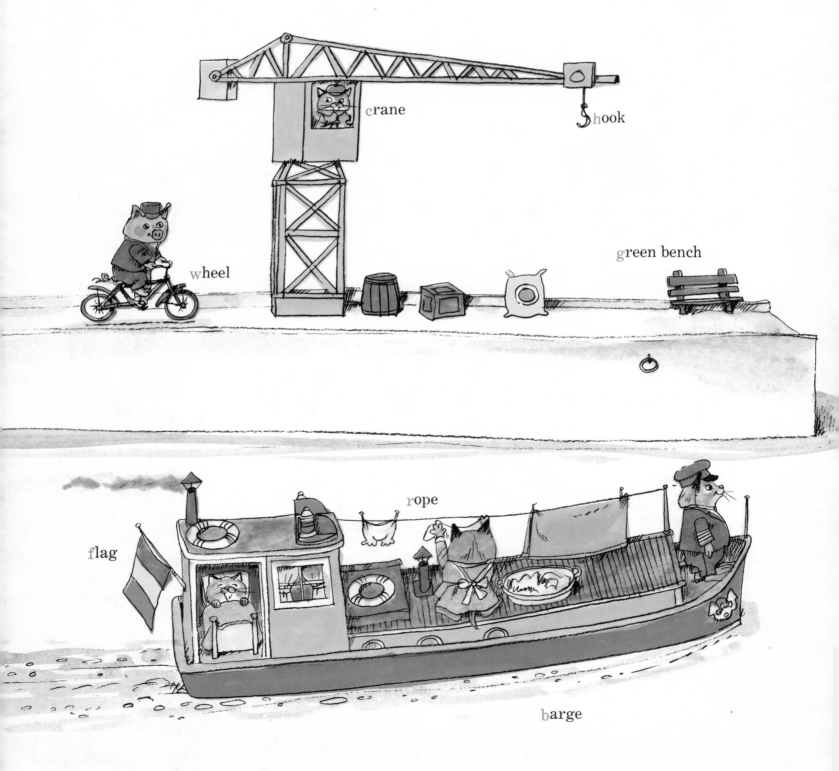

crane

hook

wheel

green bench

flag

rope

barge

Richard Scarry's ABC Word Book

parachute

bridge

car

BARBER

B.

yacht

mouse

fisherman

Collins Glasgow and London

submarine

locomotive

First published in this edition 1972
Sixth impression 1976
Published by William Collins Sons and Company Limited
Glasgow and London
© 1971 Richard Scarry
All rights reserved under International and
Pan-American Copyright Conventions
Printed in Great Britain
ISBN 0 00 138147 4

Aa

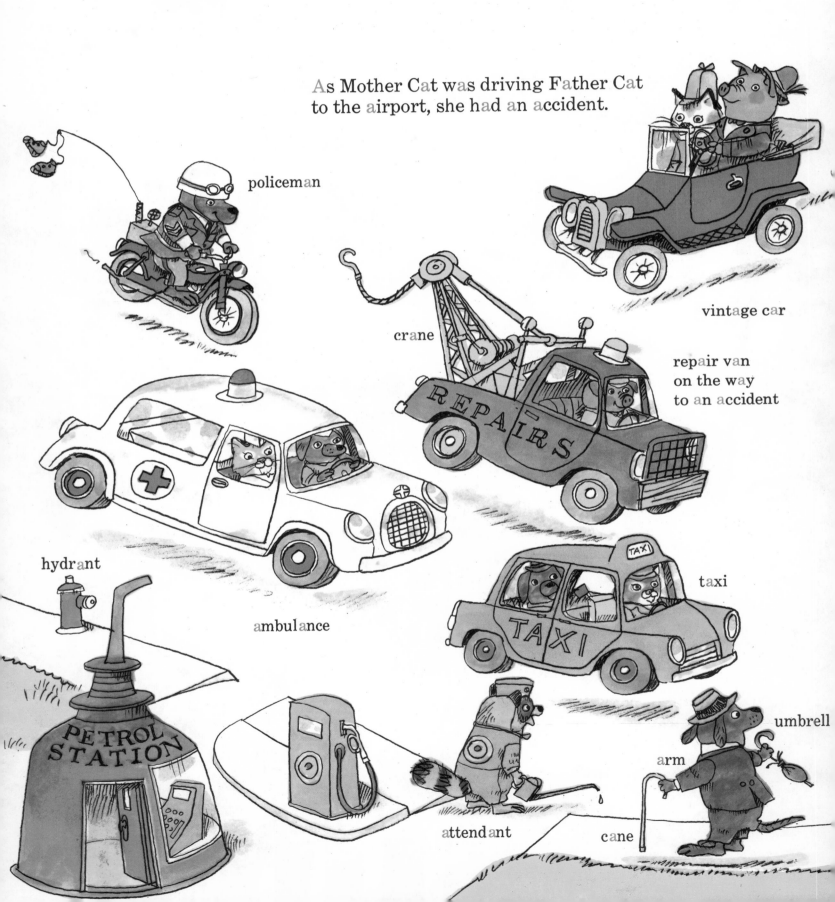

As Mother Cat was driving Father Cat to the airport, she had an accident.

policeman

vintage car

crane

repair van
on the way
to an accident

ambulance

hydrant

taxi

PETROL
STATION

attendant

arm

cane

umbrell

farmer

hat

hay cart

a racing car going fast

tractor

AIR MAIL

MAIL

REFUSE REMOVAL

The dustbin man
has a flat tyre.
He is sad.

DANGER

jack

flat tyre

sack of potatoes

bag of asparagus

basket of apples

traffic signal

manhole

ABC FARM

farm truck

CRASH!

PARKING

car

No one was hurt in the accident because
everybody was wearing a seatbelt.

baby pram

pavement

7

Aa

tail

wind vane

stewardess

hangar

boarding stairs

tramp

Father Cat

a flat rabbit

FOLLOW ME

At the airport a plane is about to land all alone. The aviator is landing by parachute.

Hilda running out of the way to safety

parachute

flag

a gay balloon

anchor

SWISSAIR

radar nose

fuel tank

landing gear

a bear asleep
in the shade

FUEL

fuel-tank lorry

luggage wagon

bag   bag   ba

A gang of ants rushing away fast

Watch out! Mother Cat!
Step on the accelerator!

water jar

artist

paint brush

9

Bb

boom

cab

banana boat

barrel

box

bag

bench

broken net

a bunch of bananas

My, what a busy harbour
with boats all about.

sightseeing boat

blanket

barge

bell

bell buoy

bumper

tugboat

tub

a raised bridge

a brick building

sailing-boat

BARBER

BAKERY

bicycle

boy

bobber

tuba

submarine

Captain Salty waves from the bridge of his big, blue ship.

radio cabin

book

blouse

brush

broom

boot

bottle

boat bottom

Cc

A **c**rowd **c**ame to Tiger **C**at's pi**c**ni**c**. Everyone li**c**ked i**c**e-**c**ream **c**ones and dan**c**ed to the lively musi**c**.

ice-cream cone

cup

A **c**ouple of mi**c**e served **c**ider from a **c**ement mixer.

a **c**ook's **c**ap

Tiger **C**at **c**ooked pop**c**orn. The **c**over wasn't **c**losed. *Crackle! Crackle! Pop!* Be **c**areful, Tiger **C**at!

packet

POP CORN

cover

can

coffeepot

camp stove

can opener

Rudolf cracked up.

cornet

camera

Crab caught popcorn in his claws.

accordion

Lowly danced in a circle with a piece of celery.

candle

Clarence couldn't count the biscuits that he ate.

What a crazy, cuckoo picnic!

Curly Pig accidentally fell into the centre of the cake. CRASH!

Ch ch

It is a chilly day, but everyone is
full of good cheer. Christmas is tomorrow
The bells chime in the church steeple.

church

a chimney sweep
scratching his itchy chin

CHOICE
and
CHEAP
MEAT
CHARLES CHIMP

The yule log is attached
to the sled with a chain.

butcher

latch

chickens

chimney

children carolling

kerchief

patch

Ma Pig is chatting with Mrs. Chipmunk.
She is also burning the chop for her
chubby children's lunch.
She is a champion chatterbox.

china

chair

stitch

bench

match

wristwatch

15

D d

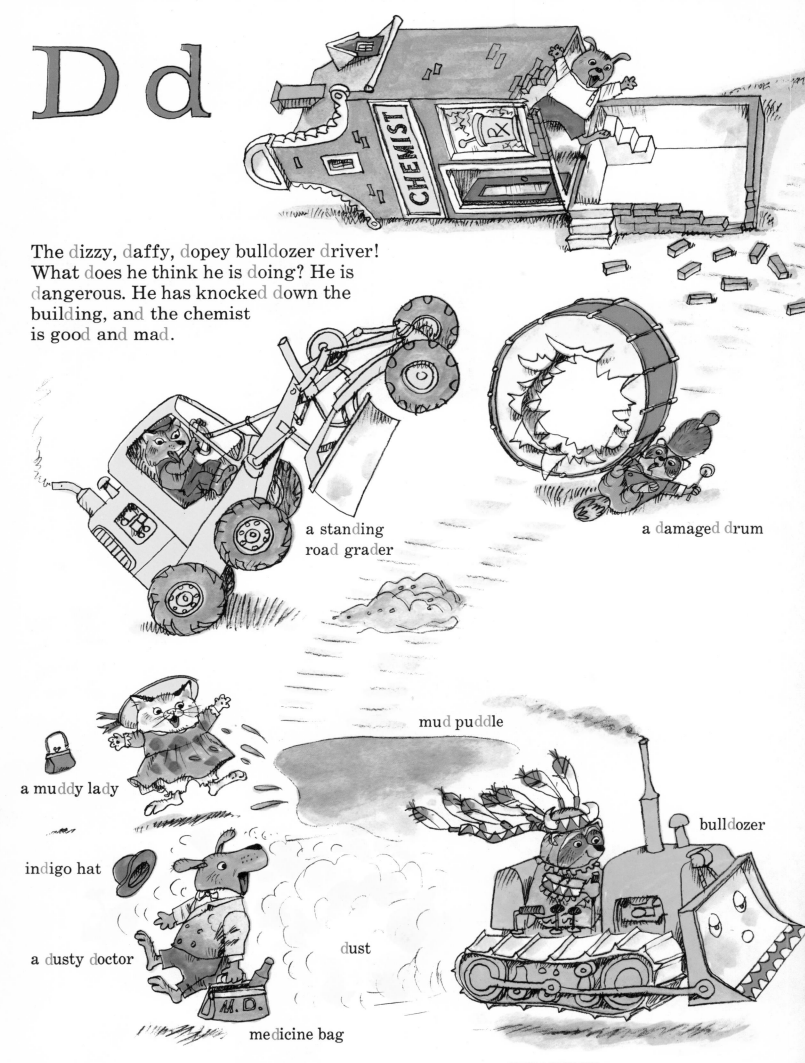

The dizzy, daffy, dopey bulldozer driver! What does he think he is doing? He is dangerous. He has knocked down the building, and the chemist is good and mad.

a standing road grader

a damaged drum

mud puddle

a muddy lady

indigo hat

a dusty doctor

dust

bulldozer

medicine bag

Wild Bill Hiccup

16

DETOUR

a dumped-over dumping lorry

dirt

derrick

board

drill

a scared ditch-digger

Where is Huckle hiding?

ladder

a deep ditch

DANGER

door

a dozen doughnuts

DOUGHNUTS

delivery man

17

E e

Ernie Elephant and his excellent firemen have just driven up to extinguish an enormous fire. Mother Rabbit is screaming for help. Do not fear! They will save her.

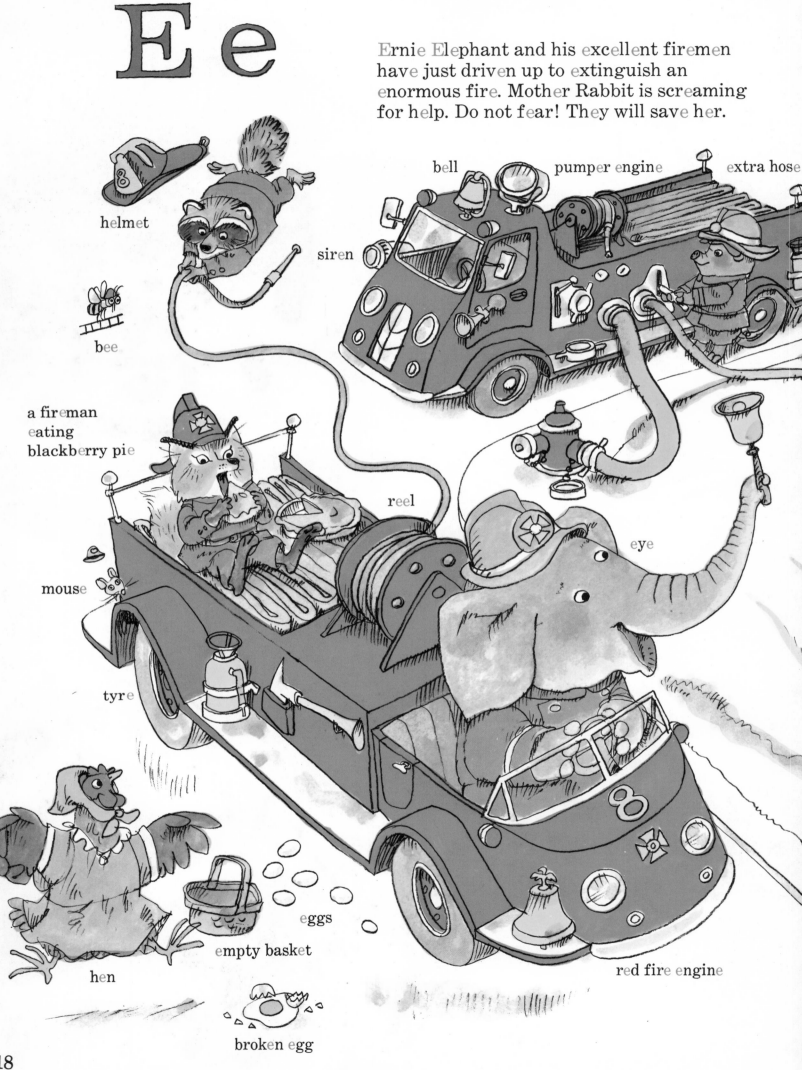

helmet

bee

siren

bell

pumper engine

extra hose

a fireman eating blackberry pie

reel

eye

mouse

tyre

hen

empty basket

eggs

red fire engine

broken egg

18

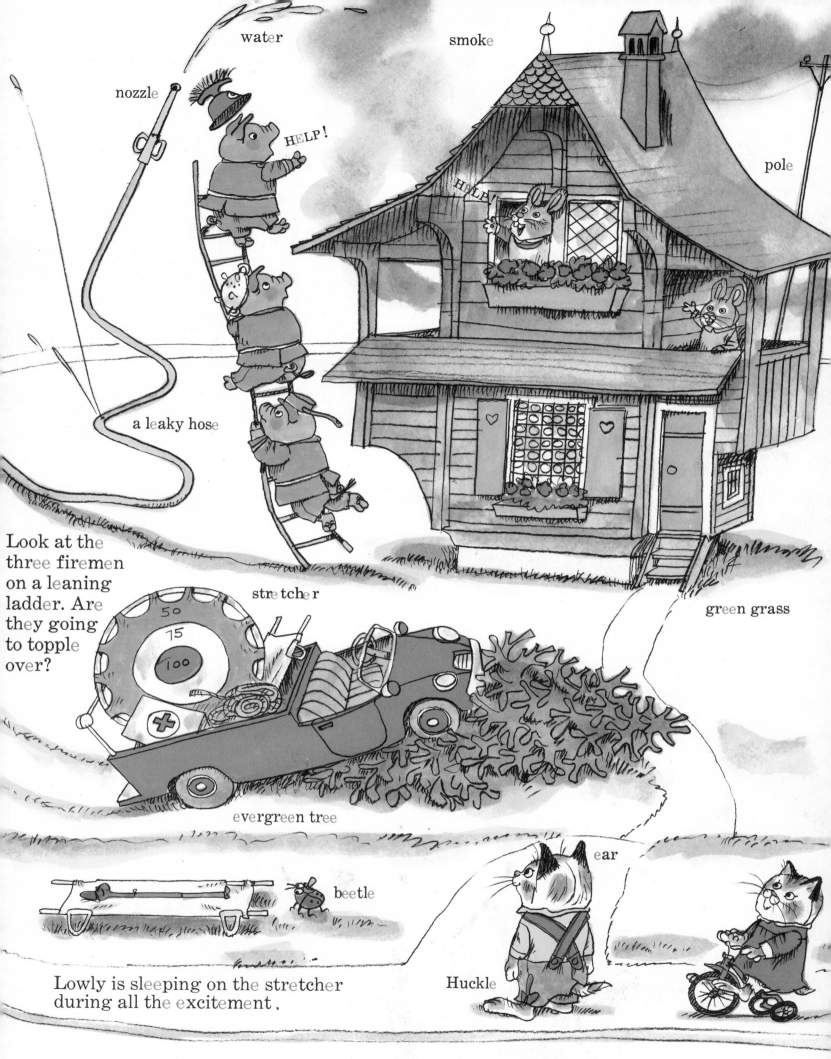

water

smoke

nozzle

HELP!

HELP!

pole

a leaky hose

Look at the three firemen on a leaning ladder. Are they going to topple over?

stretcher

50

75

100

green grass

evergreen tree

ear

beetle

Huckle

Lowly is sleeping on the stretcher during all the excitement.

street

19

Ff

a fast freight train

leaf

giraffe

a fruit tree

fence

fertilizer

field

Farmer Fox grows food in his fields for his family. There are five furry foxes hiding in the farmhouse. Can you find them?

front wheels

three frankfurters

a funny face

20

flag

farmhouse roof

forest

flower

flow

fireplace

flames

muffins

flour

floor

one fly

Five flies follow each
other in a single file.

a fat fish

Huckle fell flat
on his face.

foot

four fish

Wolf and his
friend Freddy Frog

a floating cap

knife

G g

GREASY GEORGE'S GORGEOUS GARAGE

What is going on at Greasy George's garage?

a great big green lorry

GOOD PETROL

girl

green pump

GOOD PETROL

bag

hot dog

grill

a guitar string

Goofy Goose is going to take
a group of gabby goslings to
the picnic grounds. Ugh!
He is groaning at the thought.

GO RIGHT

a midget car

22

a gardener by a glass greenhouse

a vegetable garden

The telephone is ringing *B-r-r-i-n-g-g-g!*

Grandma is grinning and giggling.

glasses

globs of grease

Greasy George is greasing a car with his grease gun. He is wearing gloves.

detergent

sponge

glue

bang!
clang!

Something is wrong here, but the mechanic is fixing it.

CAR WASH INSIDE AND OUTSIDE

BARGAIN SALE

Huckle is wearing racing goggles.

23

H h

Here is a happy home.
However, someone is unhappy.
Father hired a helper to fix
the roof shingles and the helper
hit his thumb with the hammer.
"OUCH!" he howled.

a head poking through a hole in a hat

heart

shutter

children

hatchet

hoe

Ha-ha!

Huckle has
a *very* high hat on
his head and a horn in his hands.
He is blowing hard.

hose

a hard rock

24

a helicopter hovering high above the earth

a tree house

branch

shade

Someone is hiding
in a heap of clothes.

hook

hanger

hot water

shower

Hurry, Mother! Something is
happening to the spaghetti.

honey

pitcher

dish

ketchup

a hen in
a hurry

bush

Father is digging a hole
in which to plant a bush

wheelbarrow

shovel

hole

25

I i

It is a very windy day.
The sails of the windmill were
spinning around fast until Uncle
Irving's kite string tied them up.
The miller is furious. He has
an important order to fill.

Rudolf's diving high-flyer
lost its wings in flight.
Rudolf is going swimming
with his friends.

a high hill

pipe

Willy, a little imp,
is licking an ice-cream
cone and spilling it on
Uncle Irving's shirt.

wire fence

cliff

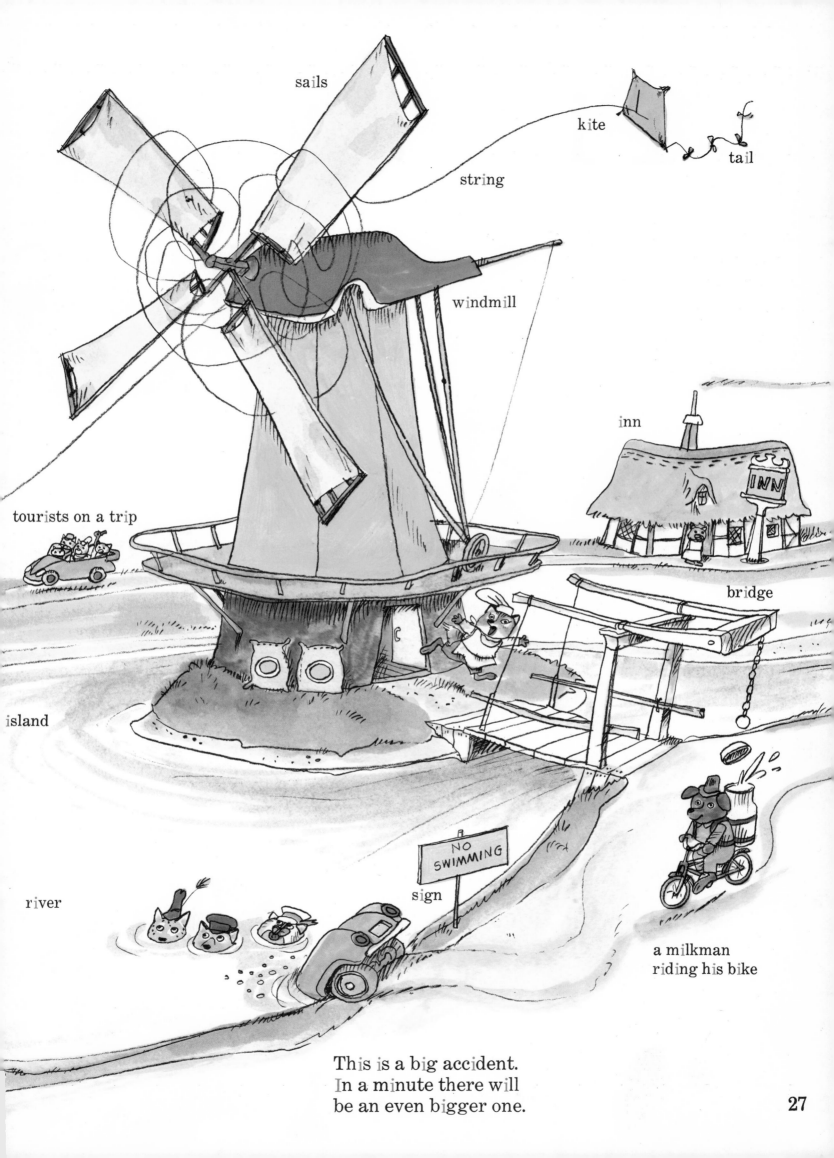

sails

kite

string

tail

windmill

inn

tourists on a trip

INN

bridge

island

NO SWIMMING

sign

river

a milkman
riding his bike

This is a big accident.
In a minute there will
be an even bigger one.

27

J j

jungle gym

Hilda just jammed a grapefruit
between her jaws and went *c-r-u-n-c-h*.
Was it juicy, Hilda?

jaw

jewel

jug

pyjamas

jumping Jill

jumbo-sized lantern

28

a jet pilot on a joy-ride

parachute jumper

Janitor Joe enjoys
driving his jeep.

This juggler
is juggling
jars of jam.

jacket

A joyful jester is playing
jolly jingles on his banjo.

K k

The king is having a snack.
He is licking a gherkin.
Kangaroo is skating in with
a cake she has baked for the king.
Would you like to share his snack?

a turkey soaking
in the sink

Duck likes to drink milk.

king

gherkin

napkin

fork

key

pocket

baked bricks

a basket of crackers

sock

broken leg

Kitten is
sucking milk
through a straw.

The cuckoo clock goes *tick-tock*.

back door

keyhole

a mouse peeking through a crack

ketchup

kettle

stick

cook book

cook

a thick steak

a leaky bucket

kangaroo

a kiss

smack!

skate

pumpkin

truck

Huckle has a pumpkin in the back of his truck.

31

Ll

A large steamroller is rolling wildly over the land. Look out, all you people, or you will be flattened!

signal light

a leaning sign

a flat limousine

The postman slipped and lost a lot of letters.

a flat bicycle

towel

a flat lawn mower

a little girl licking a lollipop

Mrs. Pig is losing her clean laundry. She calls out loudly, "Let go of my laundry! And please leave my lovely flowers alone."

oil barrel

leap frog

telephone pole

a load of long logs

bell

locomotive

a lazy fellow lying by the railway line

shovel

POLICE

a field of flat lettuce

A blue police car is
following the silly gorilla
in the steamroller.

clothes line

Huckle and Lowly!
What are you doing
with that loony gorilla?

a tall lily plant

a yellow steamroller

33

M m

trombone

drum

mouse

midget car

merry firemen making music

cement mixer

ambulance

medicine

instruments

ice-cream man

bump!

Doctor Monday on a bumpy road

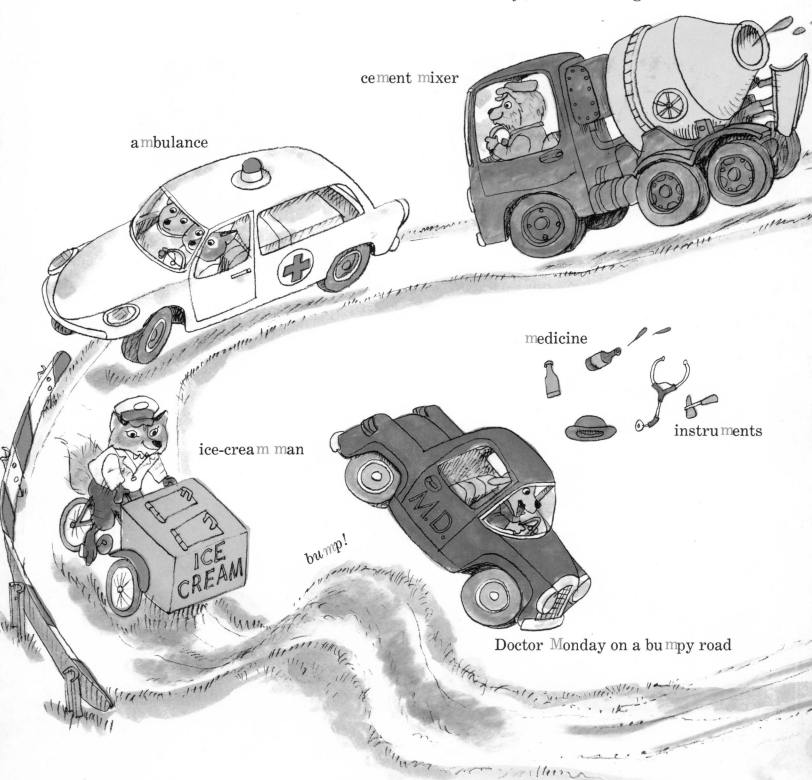

34

mail van

milk lorry

mirror

bumper

monument

WILLIAM TELL

motorcycle

smoke

PLUMBER

plumber's van

Something is the matter
with Mummy's motor.
A mechanic is trying
to make it go.
Father Pig is stuck
in the messy, muddy road.
How mad he is! Oh, my!

a messy, muddy road

SPEED
LIMIT
60
M.P.H.

Nn

aeroplane

orange crane

nose

Rudolf's plane landed in a pond.
A crane yanked it out.

a broken fence

net

a bunch of bananas

a nice nursemaid
and an infant napping

HIGH STREET

sign

a policeman running

another runner
in pink pants

nine pine trees in a long lorry

pennant

balloon

a shining sun

anchor

Another aeroplane landed in the pond—and then another.
No more, please. That is certainly enough!

newspaper

NEWS STAND

bench

a new tie

Uncle Ned

a painter painting lines

a convertible
on a saloon
on a station wagon

TREE
NURSERY

hydrant

NO
PARKING

Oh, my! See how many people have come down
to the harbour to see the boats dock.

lookout

boy

motorboat

boat

Captain
Fox

toot!

horn

pilot house

buoy

bow

portholes

Sailor Dog overboard!

rose

rowing-boat

octopus

good-bye!

hello!

oar

top

bottle

bottom

codfish
in oilskins

boots

sole

38

GOOD FOOD SHOP

trolley bus

road

Lowly Worm

an old goat looking out of a window

a young goat not looking where he is going

window

O.K. HOTEL

owl tossing a rope

bow

arrow

pole

soldier in armour

tower

Someone forgot to stop. The boat is going down to the bottom of the harbour.

clock

shore

wagon

cannon

old fort

ogre in dungeon

39

P p

Pretty Polly Pig is having a party.
She is playing the piano. *Plink! Plink!*
All the people are happy.

palm

piano

pot

trumpet

plump pig

pin

platform

Porcupine goes
poo-poo-pa-doo
on his saxophone.

bagpipe

plaid

piccolo

sharp
points

parrot

penguin

pelican
eating
peanuts

puffin

present

40

peach

pineapple

pear

a person
peeling apples
up in a lamp

Peter is pushing Paul.
Stop that, Peter.
Don't be a pest!

plate

carpet

a group of pigs

Huckle slips and
drops the plum pudding.
Lowly jumps up and
catches it.
Put it back on
the plate, Lowly!

Little Sister
pours pink punch
from a pint jug
into a paper cup.
Don't spill, please.

plop!

teapot

pie

punch bowl

41

Q q

The Queen is playing croquet with her friends.
They seem to be quarreling. Please! Let's be quiet!

The queen in her quilted robe

Two squirrels are playing quoits.

Quit it!

Quincy squeezes his water gun and water squirts out.

It hits a squid in his aquarium.

Quite a nice shot, Queenie!

Two girls play hopscotch on numbered squares.

mosquito

a quart of milk

7 8

6

4 5

3

2

1

Rr

G-r-r-r!

rabbit ear

rudder

rowing-boat

- pirate

raft

The Rapid Rabbits were racing the River Rascals in a rowing-boat race up the river. The steerer steered right onto a rock. *C-r-u-n-c-h!*
The race was over. He was in a furious rage.

drowning Lowly Worm

Huckle rescuing a swimmer

umbrella

Bravo!

Rhinoceros is rather peculiar. He prefers not to get wet when he goes into the water.

raincoat

a hungry beggar wearing rags

rubber boots

reeds

ribbon

radio

a tired
rower
resting

carrot

rock

the losers

the winners

A rooster can crow.
Can a crow rooster?

rope

water ski

raccoon

★ ★ ★
THREE STAR
RESTAURANT

terrace

REST
ROOM
→

A waiter is carrying a tray of fruit
to a customer. Who left that chair
where someone would surely trip over it?

very bad manners

45

S s

brush

smack!

stilts

scooter

Daddy Pig came into the house and kissed Mummy.

"What's for supper?" he asked.

"Your seven silly cousins are visiting us for several days," answered Mummy. "They wish to cook and serve our meals to us. They are making a super surprise supper now."

"Something does smell delicious," said Daddy. "Let's see what it is that smells so good."

Oh! Such a sight they saw!

Sam was washing dishes in the sink.

switch

soup bowl

sieve

Silas was searching for some stockings in the storage barrel.

sock

saucer

spoon

glass

sink

smash!

steam

sauce

SoAP

sponge

stick

Sandy was adding soap and sticky syrup to the stew.

Sidney was slowly stirring the stew.

sack

Stanley was spilling a strainer of slippery spaghetti.

Simon was pouring sweet strawberries into the simmering soup.

sausages

sailing-boat

sandwich

scissors

sugar

salt

Sylvester was slicing and tossing salami.

I hope everyone's stomach will be satisfied with this super surprise supper!

Sh sh

shade

shaving brush

shell

shelf

sharp shears

a shoulder shawl

wash tub

shoe

What a shame! Mother Bear washed a shirt
and it shrank. Father Bear is blushing with embarrassment.

washing-line

a sheet with shapes shaking inside it

48

shampoo

splish!

splash!

splosh!

shower

a shaggy
mop

mashed potatoes

A sheep in shabby clothes crashed through
the door to show what his brushes could do.
One could even turn on the shower!
Mother told him to shut the door.
The cold air was making her shiver.

Children were dashing and
rushing about, shrieking and
shouting, pushing and shoving.
Hush, shildren! Be shilent!
I mean, Hush, children! Be silent!

49

T t

Take a look at the terrible accident. A train has hit a truck that contained ten thousand tomatoes. What a sight!

signal tower

conductor

tickets

tracks

terrified travellers on a train trip

kite

treetop

tennis racket

net

rabbit

tennis court

tree trunk

a turtle in a tub of hot bath water

towel

string

a toad tootling on a toadstool

tow truck

trumpet

smokestack

tomatoes

tyres

tennis ball

a crossing gate torn in two

truck

tent

pot

street

tyre tracks

television set

lantern

table

tepee

Little Sister riding her tricycle

rut

Rudolf returned to earth too fast and left a great rut in the dirt. Look! You're on television, Rudolf!

51

Th th

King Theodore Thaddeus walked down the path
without thinking whither he was going.
He walked into a thicket of thistles.

thistles

Thrashing about, he found he was stuck to them.
This, he thought, is a terrible thing!
Then he threw off his thick cloth suit,
and in three seconds he was free.

However, the weather was cold,
and all he had on were thin underthings.
It is not healthy to wear nothing but that in the cold.

52

scythe

Just then Thelma, a nice lady, came along.
"WHAT ON EARTH!" she said. "Something must be done."

She cut some straw with her scythe.
Then she put a thimble on her thumb,
and with her needle and thread she made
Theodore Thaddeus a new suit of straw thatch.
King Theodore Thaddeus thanked Thelma
a thousand times.

They went back to his castle together,
and sat within before the hearth.
Then King Theodore Thaddeus thought...
Why not?
Right then and there he asked Thelma to be his
queen and share his throne with him.
Thelma was breathless.
Nevertheless...
she said "YES!"
What do you think of that!

hearth

Uu

house

When rain pours down, the ground turns to mud. Uncle Louie's car has sunk under the surface. Tough luck, Louie!

The sound of music is coming from upstairs.

Huckle playing a flute

Lowly playing a huge tuba

Crunch! Munch! Hilda is eating her lunch outside the house. Down below, a bulldozer is stuck in the muck.

Paul is pulling and grunting. Ugh!

You, there! Hurry up and shut the door before the house is full of mud.

Paddy is pushing.

underwear

Even Rudolf has put up his umbrella. Too bad he is upside down.

Aunt Ursula is jumping home after buying enough sausages for supper.

BUTCHER

Duck is busy unloading nuts out of his dump truck.

nuts

FOURTH AVENUE

Sergeant Murphy is shouting loudly, "Don't clutter up the avenue!"

a muddy uniform

55

V v

aviator

weather vane

glove

A **v**intage car is driving through a villa[ge]
and over a **v**ery high **v**iaduct. This
ro**v**ing family is going to **v**isit relatives

VILLAGE OF LOVE

two chatting wives

viaduct

a van with five
jugs of vinegar

1 2 3 4 5

a violent driver

river

a brave cat diving
to save a mouse

volcano

violets

grape vines

Vincent lives in a cave.
He is shaving his
lovely face.

a jolly violin player

Victor, the Viking, is arriving home
in his sailing vessel after a very long voyage.

W w

The weather is wild and windy.
The whole town is blowing away.

wig

walrus

a window washer
wiping a window

Lowly Worm
inside a watermelon

woods

water

a waiter losing
his warm stew

Wait!

paw

wrist watch

Wolf howling
at his hat

Huckle wearing
a weight to hold
him down

a whirring,
twirling windmill

a wet towel

a wool sweater

Owl growing wheat
in a meadow

wrench

a girl watching
at the window

a witch in
a wheelbarrow

a new
wooden wagon

wheel

two fowl squawking

two wiggling
wrestlers

a walnut on a wall

X x

axe

A fox and an ox are mixing
alphabet soup in a box.
It is excellent exercise.

exhaust

There are exactly six saxophone
players in the taxi.

Y y

Yak is playing
with his Yo-Yo.

Why is the roly-poly pig
crying? He has his own toy.

yacht

Z z

Z-Z-Z-O-O-M!

a hat that is
the wrong size

bulldozer

blazer

a zebra in
a zipper jacket

chimpanzee

Lowly is snoozing.

razzle dazzle
exit
nix
yoo hoo

tin lizzie

a dozing baby

buzzer

Yellow stripes show
the safety zone.

Izzy Lizard is dizzy. He is walking zigzag.

Aa Bb Cc

Gg Hh Ii

Mm Nn Oo

Ss Tt Uu

Xx Yy